# MASTERING THE ART OF CUNNILINGUS (ORAL SEX)

## GUIDE TO GIVING HEAD LIKE A PRO

**Jane Lawrence**

# Contents

# INTRODUCTION

The Secrets of Great Sex books are compact manuals that focus on only the most important material. Whether you want to try a new sex position, want to know how to achieve true closeness, or want to know how to pleasure your spouse, there's a Secrets of Great Sex book for you!

Yes, sex is a natural, biological activity as old as humanity, but for many individuals, particularly those who are self-conscious in the bedroom, sex (at least good sex) may not come readily.

If you are scared, apprehensive, self-conscious, or otherwise distracted, sex is unlikely to be enjoyable.

The good news is that having excellent sex isn't an insurmountable task. It may be far more achievable than you believe. It may need some work and practice (which I guarantee will be enjoyable!). But before you know it, your sex life will be greater than you could have ever imagined.

Exploring and learning about our sexual nature comes naturally to some people but appears difficult to many others. We aren't taught much about sen unless we have parents who aren't scared to talk about it. Young kids learn about sex through peer pressure and experimentation.

The older a person grows before having had sexual contact, the more unprepared that person would feel when entering a sexual relationship.

It becomes an amazing experience when we are well-informed, practiced, and eager about sex. We are born with all of the necessary sexual equipment. What we need is a type of "owner's manual"—a guide to help us learn, ideas to try with, and rules to let us know we're on the right track.

Every partnership is unique, as are their sexual encounters. It may not seem that different right now, but as you discover more about your sexual nature, you will notice distinctions each time you make love. This will provide you with a foundation from which to grow even higher.

Being conscious but not self-conscious when having sex is the key to making each encounter feel new and exciting, and we are all accountable for our sexual bliss. It is not our lover's obligation, however, it is nice to be coupled with someone who desires sexual satisfaction as well.

"Mastering The Art Of Cunnilingus" is intended to provide you with all of the tools you need to achieve a complete, gratifying, and expanded sexual and sensual experience.

These guidelines will keep you informed for many years to come and will offer you the insight and information you need for a wonderful sexual future. A long life, a healthy life, a happy life, and a fantastic sex life all go hand in hand.

# Chapter 1

## CUNNILINGUS

What exactly is Cunnilingus?
"Cunnilingus is oral sex done on a vulva and/or vagina," says Wikipedia. "Any combination of mouth and tongue on the vulva and/or vagina can be included."

This includes sucking, licking, flicking, nibbling, biting, and other activities.

While cunnilingus is the formal term for oral-vulvar sex, the act has several vernacular nicknames. These include mentioning a few, licking the bean, 3rd base, and eating out.
According to a study, women increasingly prefer oral sex above any other sort of sexual activity. This is

because cunnilingus has become a popular sexual practice, indicating a shift in the tide of sexual behavior.

This sexual practice is becoming more prevalent among young women and is an important aspect of the sexual revolution of the twenty-first century. The majority of women who engaged in oral sex did so because they loved it. Almost a third stated they liked providing fellatio because it made them feel powerful.

What kind of women like oral sex? It's hardly unexpected that it's more popular among women who have high sexual self-esteem. Researchers discovered that women who have a good attitude about their genitals had more sex and enjoy it more than others. Those who have a negative attitude toward their genitals, on the other hand, experience less pleasure from cunnilingus (Reinholtz & Muehlenhard, 1995, psychworld.com).

Why do women enjoy receiving dental care?

Simply, it does the job. Around 70% of women can only orgasm if their clitoris is stroked directly with their lips, tongue, fingers, or things such as vibrators, whereas the remaining 30% can climax through vaginal intercourse. Although this is a contentious issue, most sexologists feel that the clit is the cause of all female orgasms. Women, on the other hand, can climax during vaginal intercourse if their clitoris is additionally stimulated by the posture chosen (The

Grind is one of the best-known positions for this).

Oral sex, on the other hand, is a safer bet. The tongue is very popular since it is soft and warm, and saliva is a natural lubricant that avoids 'burn' from dry stimulation. The more aroused a woman is from foreplay, the simpler it is for her to climax in oral play since the vaginal area becomes progressively engorged with blood the more she's turned on.

Oral offers more orgasmic possibilities. Women require continuous, consistent stimulation to have an orgasm, which requires the giver to be patient and not rush. Guys normally climax more rapidly during vaginal intercourse because of the stimulation this offers the penis - and women typically require stimulation for a longer amount of time than their partners can last.

Because there are no distractions, such as his imminent orgasm, the giver is more likely to offer the correct sort of stimulation in the cunnilingus. The provider can also stimulate many locations at the same time with her hands and lips; multiple stimulations are more likely to push a woman over the point of no return. And if his tongue becomes tired, he may easily maintain the pleasure strokes with his fingers or a vibrator.

Even if a woman does not climax from oral play, if she is near, vaginal intercourse may offer the final push over the brink - especially in a sex position that rubs the G-spot or delivers dual vaginal/clitoral stimulation.

Pleasuring a woman orally is increasingly likely to take center stage as the understanding of women's sexual response develops, particularly since stimulating the clitoris is the single most essential pathway to female orgasms.

# Chapter 2

## How to Do Cunnilingus

The majority of vulva owners have been brainwashed to believe that their vulvas are filthy and unsightly.

Appreciating their body verbally before diving in might assist boost their confidence and comfort level while receiving.

Are they lovely? Do they have a pleasant odor? Do you want to try them? Inform them.

Pre-play, like penetrative sex, goes a long way. Why not begin with a kiss on the neck or lips and work your way down their complete body?

You'll get to the ears, fingers, nipples, navel, lower stomach, and inner thighs, among other erogenous zones.

A decent rule of thumb is to take three times as long as you think you need to get to the real oral sex.

Is the position important?
Cunnilingus prefers missionary oral, with the receiving partner on their back.

If it hurts your neck, place a cushion beneath your partner's hips to raise them. Alternatively, have them slide to the edge of the bed and squat in front of them.

Facesitting and 69 (or slanted 69) are other possibilities.

"Just make sure you're both comfortable so you can enjoy it."

Clothing Or No Clothing?
It's great to tease your spouse through their underwear and lick along the seams. If your partner's clit is very sensitive, this may be their preference.

You'll both probably want their underwear out of the way at some point. And why is that? "Can I take these off?" you may wonder. "Are you prepared for me to taste you?"

Pull them down once you have their permission.
Cunnilingus is not a one-size-fits-all experience. Experiment with various rhythms, pressures, postures, and

motions to find out what works best for you and your present partner.

"Begin with wide, moderate pressure and work your way up," Struyk advises.

Up and down are two strategies to attempt.
Circular motion in a clockwise direction.
Circular motion in the opposite direction.
from one side to the other.
pulsing in one location.
Sucking softly while curling your mouth around the clit.
Because not everyone appreciates direct stimulation, you may wind up extremely close to — but not exactly on — the clitoris itself.

Oh, and begin slowly.

"It's simpler to ask for more than it is to beg you to back off."

How Do You Keep Your Teeth In Place?
In actuality, your chompers are not as bad as you would believe.

Worried? Lead with your tongue and use your lips to form a tiny casing around your tusks.

Can You Turn This Into A Rim Job?
Without a doubt! So long as your partner gives you the okay.

Just don't do it backward, since this can send bacteria from the anus into your partner's vagina and vulva, increasing the risk of infection.

How Do You Use Your Hands?
Don't be embarrassed; you may eat with your hands as long as your spouse agrees.

"Why leave them hanging when you might excite them more by stroking [your spouse] someplace else?"

There are many possibilities here. You may use them to play about with and tease your partner's nipples. Alternatively, use them to go into your partner's front or rear hole. Alternatively, try using them to keep your partner's hips in place as they grind on your kisser.

If your spouse prefers intravaginal stimulation, you might use your hands to access the full pleasure potential of their clitoris via their G-zone.

Insert your fingers around 2 inches inside their vagina and use rhythmic pressure to find their G-spot.

Should You Experiment with Penetration?
Only if your spouse has an interest in doing so.

Do You Need to Make Eye Contact?
Some people will close their eyes and relax into the experience while receiving. Others like the sight of their lover sandwiched between their legs.

Sloane believes that nothing is more intimate than making eye contact with a partner during oral play. Allow yourself to sometimes gaze up at your companion.

Should You Make a Sound?
Moaning on your partner's body might produce a scorching, rumbling feeling on their vulva.

Slurping, suctioning, and spitting are also acceptable (read: encouraged).

How Do You Incorporate Sex Toys?
Sloane says insertable G-spot vibrators, dildos, and butt plugs may all improve the experience, whether you hold them, your spouse holds them, or you insert them.

# Chapter 3

## Communication during oral sex

How can you tell whether your spouse likes what you're doing?
Take note of their body language.

Clues, whether vocal or nonverbal, are nonetheless cues. Pay attention to your partner's breathing patterns, how their hips lean toward or away from your lips, and what their hands are doing.

They'll let you know whether they enjoy what you're doing.

How Do You Know If You Should Continue?
If your spouse is groaning or keeping your head down, likely, they don't want you to stop. Continue doing what

you're doing as long as you're having fun.

"Don't let their enthusiasm encourage you to go faster or harder, as this may disrupt the feel-good rhythm you've developed."
If you want to quit, you should stop! Your spouse will be able to tell if you're doing cunnilingus because you believe you "should" or because you're not into it.

Some methods for getting out of oral sex include:

"I enjoy tasting you, but my mouth hurts. Is it okay if I used a toy on you instead?"
"Come on in and taste yourself off my lips."

"Would you want to utilize the air suction toy? I want to get closer to your lips and kiss you."
"You taste great, baby. But what I want is..."
What if your lover wants you to do something else?
Whether or whether your spouse has climaxed, if they are dragging you back up to their face or pushing you away, they are probably done.

Check-in to see what they want next.
A cuddling session to unwind? Persuasive sex? What about a back massage?

Remember, just because you gave them the head doesn't mean they owe you the head.

What About After Everything Is Said And Done?

Are you finished? Tell your boo how much fun you had getting down on them. Allow them to taste themselves on your lips while you tell them how much you adore their flavor.

## Conclusion

Are there any dangers associated with cunnilingus?

That is an excellent question!

Oral sex poses no risk during pregnancy. However, sexually transmitted diseases (STIs) can be transferred by oral sex.

Cunnilingus can spread Chlamydia, gonorrhea, syphilis, herpes, and possibly HIV and HPV.

Your strategy: Before going down on your lover, discuss their current STI status with them. Consider utilizing a dental dam if one or both of you are STI-positive or are ignorant of your current STI status.

A dental dam is a more secure sex aid that acts as a barrier between you and your sweetheart.

Aside from STDs and STIs, there are no significant hazards associated with oral sex as long as you practice safer sex and don't bite!